It's A Girl

Edited by Linda Sunshine
Designed by Barbara Scott-Goodman

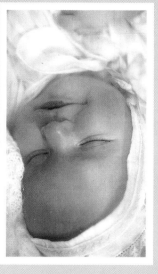

Macmillan Publishing Company
New York

Maxwell Macmillan Canada
Toronto

Maxwell Macmillan International
New York   Oxford   Singapore   Sydney

Macmillan Publishing Company
866 Third Avenue
New York, NY 10022

Maxwell Macmillan Canada, Inc.
1200 Eglinton Avenue East, Suite 200
Don Mills, Ontario M3C 3N1

Macmillan Publishing Company is part of the Maxwell Communication Group of Companies.

Library of Congress Cataloging-in-Publication Data
It's a girl / edited by Linda Sunshine.
p. cm.
Summary: An illustrated anthology of excerpts from classic children's stories, poems, songs, nursery rhymes, and novels by authors like Byron, Saki, Yeats, Lewis Carroll, and Edith Wharton.
ISBN 0-02-615401-3
1. Girls—Literary collections.   [1. Girls—Literary collections.]   I. Sunshine, Linda.
PZ5.I85   1992   91-13467
808.8'0352042—dc20   CIP
                                                                                          AC

Produced by Smallwood and Stewart, Inc., New York City

Notice: Every effort has been made to locate the copyright owners of the material used in this book. Please let us know if an error has been made, and we will make any necessary changes in subsequent printings.

Macmillan books are available at special discounts for bulk purchases for sales promotions, premiums, fund-raising, or educational use. For details, contact: Special Sales Director, Macmillan Publishing Company, 866 Third Avenue, New York, NY 10022

10 9 8 7 6 5 4 3 2 1

Printed in Singapore

INTRODUCTION

*N*othing is more sweet than a daughter," wrote Euripides, like an echo of what every parent must feel upon their birth of their own newborn girl.

Many artists, writers, and poets have attempted to describe the feeling of welcoming a newborn into the world. Marilyn French, for example, once said the emotion was ". . . somehow absolute, truer and more binding than any other experience life had to offer."

A child enters the world and the world is changed. And so this book celebrates the birth of your daughter, a magical creature. "A baby is God's opinion that the world should go on," wrote Carl Sandburg. And the world is surely a better place now that your daughter has arrived.

Linda Sunshine

To begin my life
with the beginning of my life,
I record that I was born
(as I have been informed and believe)

on . . . .

Charles Dickens
David Copperfield

Her Birthday . . . .

IT'S A GIRL

Her Name ....

Her Parents ....

Her Birthplace ....

Her Weight ....

Her Measurement ....

very baby born into the world is a finer one than the last.

Charles Dickens

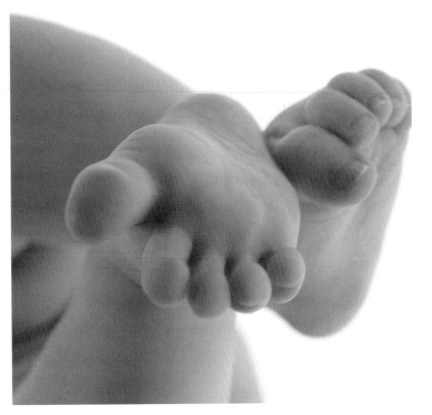

The child's foot still
doesn't know it's a foot,

it wants to be a butterfly or apple.

Pablo Neruda
To the Foot From Its Child

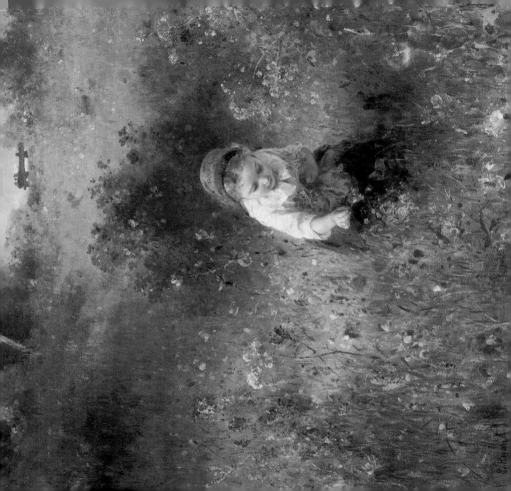

One fair daughter and no more,
The which he loved passing well.

William Shakespeare
Hamlet

learned to watch, to put my trust in other hands than mine. And I learned to wander. I learned what every dreaming child needs to know—that no horizon is so far that you cannot get above it or beyond it. These I learned at once. But most things come harder.

Beryl Markham
West With the Night

"The time has come," the Walrus said,
"to talk of many things:
Of shoes—and ships—and sealing wax—
Of cabbages—and kings . . ."

Lewis Carroll
Through the Looking Glass

_P_retty much all the
honest truth telling
there is in the world
is done by children.

Oliver Wendell Holmes

22

SHE was the most winning thing that ever brought sunshine into a desolate house—a real beauty in face—with the Earnshaws' handsome dark eyes, but the Lintons' fair skin and small features, and yellow curling hair. Her spirit was high, though not rough, and qualified by a heart, sensitive and lively to excess in its affections. That capacity for intense attachments reminded me of her mother; still she did not resemble her; for she could be soft and mild as a dove, and she had a gentle voice, and pensive expression: her anger was never furious, her love never fierce; it was deep and tender.

Emily Brontë
Wuthering Heights

Love me—I love you,
Love me, my baby;
Sing it high, sing it low,
Sing it as may be.

Mother's arms under you;
Her eyes above you;
Sing it high, sing it low.
Love me—I love you.

Christina Rossetti

All children, except one, grow up. They soon know that they will grow up, and the way Wendy knew was this. One day when she was two years old she was playing in a garden, and she plucked another flower and ran with it to her mother. I suppose she must have looked rather delightful, for Mrs. Darling put her hand to her heart and cried, 'Oh, why can't you remain like this for ever!' This was all that passed between them on the subject, but henceforth Wendy knew that she must grow up. You always know after you are two. Two is the beginning of the end.

J.M. Barrie
Peter Pan

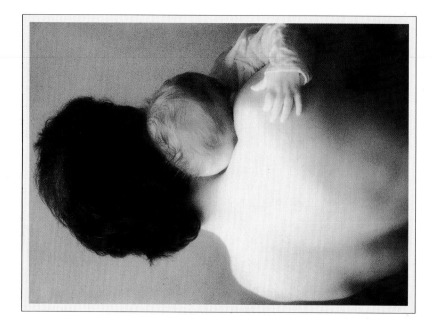

. . . . For who knows what my girl will be?
She's only a few months old, and a surprise
already—and I imagine I've got a lot more sur-
prises coming. But in the end, I suppose, I just
want to give her love and the assurance of a
home on earth. . . . She was born that I might
give her a first foot in this world and might help
her to want to live in it. She is here through me,
and I am responsible for her. . . . Having a
child alters the rights of every man, and I don't
expect to live as I did without her.

Laurie Lee
I Can't Stay Long

"And here is my sweet little Annamaria," Lady Middleton added, tenderly caressing a little girl of three years old, who had not made a noise for the last two minutes. "And she is always so gentle and quiet—never was there such a quiet little thing!"

Jane Austen
Sense and Sensibility

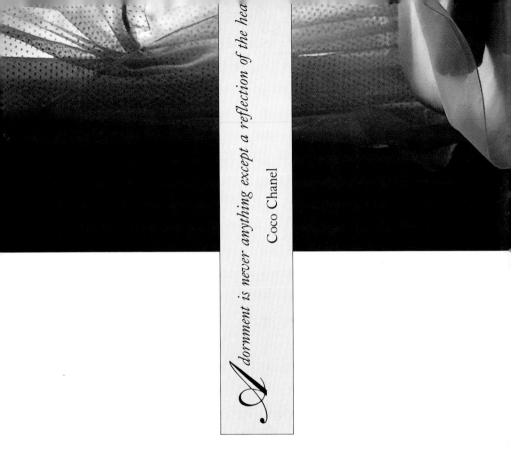

Adornment is never anything except a reflection of the hea...

Coco Chanel

She brought up her daughter Bee with the most charming wisdom. She taught this child only to take pleasure in doing good, consequently, she could indulge her to any extent.

Anatole France
Bee: Princess of the Dwarfs

Babies are such a nice way to start people.

Don Herold

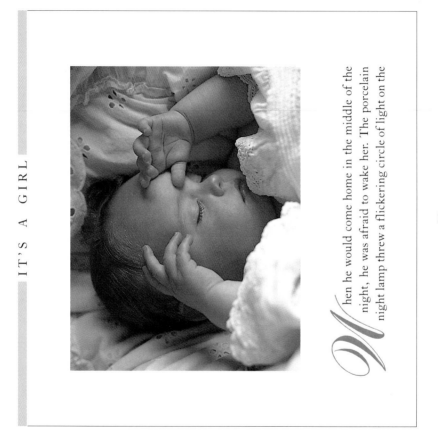

When he would come home in the middle of the night, he was afraid to wake her. The porcelain night lamp threw a flickering circle of light on the ceiling, and the drawn curtains of the small cradle were like a white tent billowing out in the dark at the edge of the bed. Charles . . . thought he could hear his daughter's gentle breathing. She was going to grow up now; each season would bring quick progress. He already saw her coming back from school in the late afternoon, laughing gaily, her blouse ink-stained, her basket dangling from her arm. . . . Ah! How pretty she would be later on, at fifteen, when, resembling her mother, she would wear great big straw hats like hers in the summertime. From afar they would be taken for sisters. He pictured her to himself near them in the evening under the lamplight. She would embroider slippers for him, busy herself with household chores, fill the whole house with her engaging ways and her gaiety. Eventually they would think about getting her settled. They would find her some fine young man with a solid business who would make her happy; It would last forever.

Gustave Flaubert

THERE

was a little girl

Who had a little curl

Right in the middle of her forehead;

And when she was good

She was very, very good,

But when she was bad she was horrid.

Henry Wadsworth Longfellow
There Was A Little Girl

Secrets with girls, like loaded guns with boys,
Are never valued till they make a noise.

George Crabbe
The Maid's Story

44

hildren in a family are
like flowers in a bouquet: there's
always one determined to face in
an opposite direction from the way
the arranger desires.

Marcelene Cox

M ay she become a flourishing hidden tree
That all her thoughts may like the linnet be,
And have no business but dispensing round
Their magnanimities of sound,
Nor but in merriment begin a chase,
Nor but in merriment a quarrel.
O may she live like some green laurel
Rooted in one dear perpetual place.

William Butler Yeats
A Prayer For My Daughter

IT'S A GIRL

The King of China's daughter,
  So beautiful to see
With her face like yellow water, left
  Her nutmeg tree.
Her little rope for skipping
  She kissed and gave it me—
Made of painted notes of singing-birds
  Among the fields of tea.
I skipped across the nutmeg grove,
  I skipped across the sea;
But neither sun nor moon, my dear,
  Has yet caught me.

Edith Sitwell
The King of China's Daughter

One's prime is elusive. You little girls, when you grow up, must be on the alert to recognize your prime at whatever time of your life it may occur.

Muriel Spark
The Prime of Miss Jean Brodie

To *an old father, nothing is more sweet*

Than a daughter:

Boys are more spirited, but their ways

Are not so tender.

Euripides

She was a dear, good little girl, who was always obedient and said her prayers before going to bed and in the morning when she got up. Everything she did went well. When she planted something in her little garden patch, a clump of violets or a sprig of rosemary, it took root so well that you could see it growing. When danger threatened the little girl, she was always saved, and the mother often thought in her heart: My child must have a guardian angel, who goes everywhere with her, even if the angel cannot be seen.

Wilhelm Grimm
Dear Mili

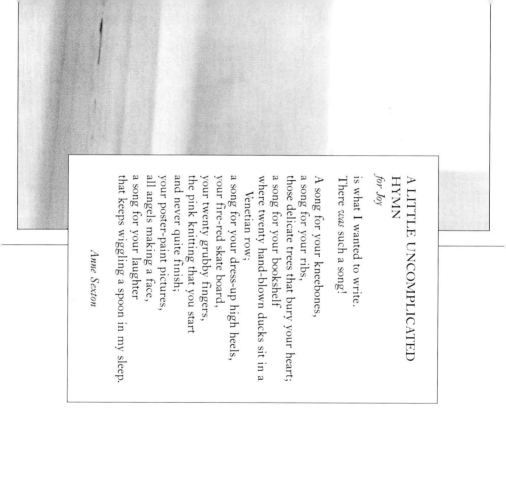

A LITTLE UNCOMPLICATED HYMN

for Joy

is what I wanted to write.
There *was* such a song!

A song for your kneebones,
a song for your ribs,
those delicate trees that bury your heart;
a song for your bookshelf
where twenty hand-blown ducks sit in a
        Venetian row;
a song for your dress-up high heels,
your fire-red skate board,
your twenty grubby fingers,
the pink knitting that you start
and never quite finish;
your poster-paint pictures,
all angels making a face,
a song for your laughter
that keeps wiggling a spoon in my sleep.

Anne Sexton

Mothers and daughters are part of each other's consciousness, in different degrees and in a different way, but still with the mutual sense of something which has always been there. A real mother is just a habit of thought to her children.

Edith Wharton
The Mother's Recompense

For Cam grazed the easel by an inch; she would not stop for Mr. Bankes and Lily Briscoe; though Mr. Bankes, who would have liked a daughter of his own, held out his hand; she would not stop for her father, whom she grazed also by an inch; nor for her mother, who called "Cam! I want you a moment!" as she dashed past. She was off like a bird, bullet, or arrow, impelled by what desire, shot by whom, at what directed, who could say? What, what? Mrs. Ramsay pondered, watching her. It might be a vision—of a shell, of a wheelbarrow, of a fairy kingdom on the far side of the hedge; or it might be the glory of speed; no one knew. But when Mrs. Ramsay called "Cam!" a second time, the projectile dropped in mid career, and Cam came lagging back, pulling a leaf by the way, to her mother.

Virginia Woolf
To the Lighthouse

**Little Girl,
My Stringbean,
My Lovely Woman**

Anne Sexton

live in gratitude to my parents for initiating me—and as early as I begged for it, without keeping me waiting—into knowledge of the word, into reading and spelling, by way of the alphabet. They taught it to me at home in time for me to begin to read before starting to school. I believe the alphabet is no longer considered an essential piece of equipment for traveling through life. In my day it was the keystone to knowledge. You learned the alphabet as you learned to count to ten, as you learned, "Now I lay me" and the Lord's Prayer and your father's and mother's name and address and telephone number, all in case you were lost.

Eudora Welty
One Writer's Beginnings

Mother, may I go out to swim?
Yes, my darling daughter:
Hang your clothes on a hickory limb
And don't go near the water.

Nursery Rhyme

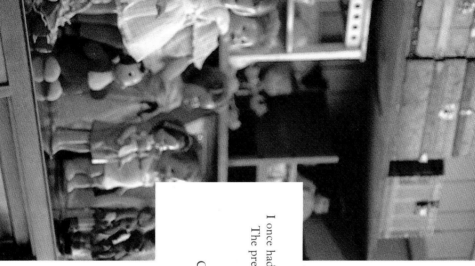

I once had a sweet little doll, dears,
The prettiest doll in the world.

❧

Charles Kingsley
My Little Doll

Ada!
Sole daughter
of my house and heart.

Lord Byron
Childe Harold's Pilgrimage

S everal years ago, I flew with my children back home to California. The afternoon of our arrival, we went for a walk along the Carmel beach. It was sunset, the beach was particularly sharp with color, and the sun hung like a fiery communion wafer on the horizon, its last rays laying a track of gold across the water to the edge of the wet sand where I stood.

Seized with the desire to impress this scene upon my children, who were skittering like sandpipers at the ocean's edge, I gathered them together and showed them how to make a frame out of their fingers to capture the sunset like a picture. They were only mildly interested in this instant photography, and after several moments they broke away to run up and down the beach again.

"Well," I thought, retreating to a sand dune and sitting down alone, "so much for a mother's metaphysics." But then I was aware that my six-year-old daughter was plunging straight into the ocean and was already up to her knees in the strong Pacific surf.

I cupped my hands and yelled, "Wait, come back!" My daughter turned around, cast a regretful look back toward the ocean and ran to where I was sitting. "It's dangerous out there," I explained. "The water is deep." She lowered herself onto the sand, put her chin upon her knees and said quietly, "But I was only trying to step on the sunset."

Phyllis Theroux
California and Other States of Grace

*hank heaven for little girls!*

For little girls get bigger every day.

Thank heaven for little girls!

They grow up in the most delightful way,

Those little eyes so helpless and appealing,

One day will flash and send you crashing through the ceiling.

Thank heaven for
little girls;

Thank heaven for them
all no matter where,
no matter who,

Without them
what would little boys do?

Alan Jay Lerner
Thank Heaven for Little Girls

Little Lucy Lavender,
Aged just three,
Dances over the water,
Dances over the sea,
Dances by the streamlet,
Dances on the hill—
Little Lucy Lavender
She can't stand still!

Little Lucy Lavender,
Aged just three,
Sang as she clambered
Up the apple tree;
Sang in her bath-tub,
Sang in her bed,
For—"I can't stay quiet,"
Little Lucy said.

Ivy O. Eastwick
Lucy Lavender

Every day I count wasted in which there has been no dancing.

Frederich Nietzsche
The Dance of Life

ortense was like her mother in appearance, but her naturally wavy and astonishingly thick hair was red gold. Her dazzling skin had the quality of pearl. It was easy to see that she was the child of a true marriage, of pure and noble love in its perfect prime. There was an ardent eagerness in her face, a gaiety in her gestures, a youthful surge of vitality, a fresh bloom of life, a vigorous good health, that seemed to vibrate in the air about her and emanate from her in electric waves. All heads turned to watch Hortense. When her sea-blue eyes with their clear limpidity of innocence rested on some passerby, he involuntarily thrilled. Moreover, her complexion was not marred by freckles, which are the price that golden-fair girls often pay for the milky whiteness of their skins. Tall, rounded without being plump, of a graceful physique as noble as her mother's, she merited the title of "goddess" that the old authors bestow so freely. No one meeting her in the street could help exclaiming: "Heavens! what a lovely girl!" She was so utterly innocent that she used to say when they came home: "How can you speak of a 'lovely girl,' Mama, when you are with me? You are surely so much lovelier than I! . . ."

Honoré de Balzac
Cousin Bette

❧

The world is so full of a number of things
I'm sure we should all be as happy as kings.

Robert Louis Stevenson
Happy Thought

And of course children are wonderful and charming creatures. I've had Ann in talking about the white seal and wanting me to read to her. And how Karin manages to be so aloof I can't think. There's a quality in their minds to me very adorable; to be alone with them, and see them day by day would be an extraordinary experience. They have what no grown up has—that directness—chatter, chatter, chatter, on Ann goes, in a kind of world of her own, with its seals and dogs; happy because she's going to have cocoa tonight, and go blackberrying tomorrow. The walls of her mind are all hung round with such bright vivid things, and she doesn't see what we see.

Virginia Woolf
A Writer's Diary

*T*he summer that I was ten—
Can it be there was only one
summer when I was ten?

May Swenson
The Centaur

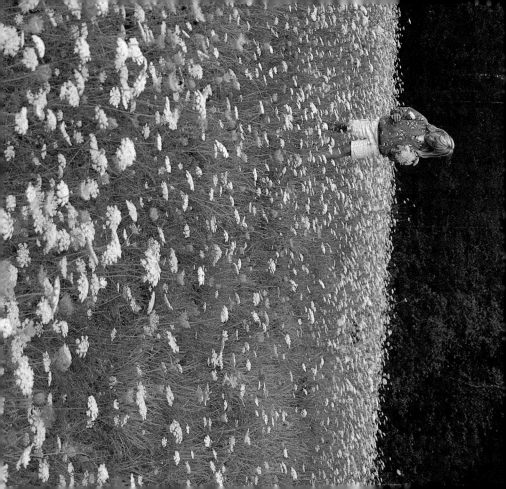

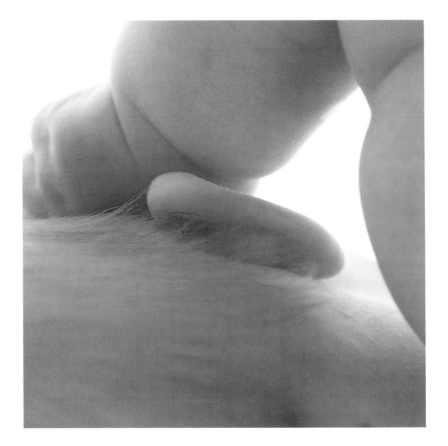

A baby is God's opinion that the world should go on.

Carl Sandburg

Later on, when they had all said "Good-bye" and "Thank you" to Christopher Robin, Pooh and Piglet walked home thoughtfully together in the golden evening, and for a long time they were silent.

"When you wake up in the morning, Pooh," said Piglet at last, "what's the first thing you say to yourself?"

"What's for breakfast?" said Pooh. "What do you say, Piglet?"

"I say, I wonder what's going to happen exciting *today*?" said Piglet.

Pooh nodded thoughtfully. "It's the same thing," he said.

A. A. Milne
Winnie-the-Pooh

❦

❦

"Good night, little girls!
Thank the Lord you are well!
And now go to sleep!"
said Miss Clavel.

And she turned out the light
and closed the door—
and that's all there is—
There isn't any more.

Ludwig Bemelmans
Madeline

PERMISSIONS
AND PHOTO CREDITS

COVER: Photograph by Monica Roberts

8: Photograph by Monica Roberts.

10-11: Photograph by Barbara Campbell.

12: Photograph by Penny Gentieu.

13: "To the Foot From Its Child" in *Five Decades: Poems 1925-1970* by Pablo Neruda, translated by Ben Belitt. Copyright © 1961 by Ben Belitt. Used by permission of Grove Press, Inc.

14-15: "A Young Girl in a Field" by Ludwig Knaus. Reprinted with permission of The Bridgeman Art Library, Limited.

16: Photograph by Monica Roberts.

17: Excerpted from *West With the Night*, copyright © 1983 by Beryl Markham. Published by North Point Press and reprinted by permission.

18-19: Photograph by Monica Roberts.

21: Photograph by Monica Roberts.

22: "Pontus 1890" by Carl Larsson. Reprinted with permission of The Bridgeman Art Library, Limited.

25: Photograph by Monica Roberts.

26-27: Photograph by Monica Roberts. Excerpt reprinted with permission of Charles Scribner's Sons, an imprint of Macmillan Publishing Company from *Peter Pan* by James M. Barrie. Copyright 1911, 1921 Charles Scribner's Sons; copyrights renewed 1939, 1949 Lady Cynthia Asquith and Peter L. Davies.

28: Photograph by Marcia Lippman.

29: Excerpt from *I Can't Stay Long* by Laurie Lee, reprinted by permission of Andre Deutsch Ltd. Copyright © 1975 Laurie Lee.

65: Excerpt from *One Writer's Beginnings* by Eudora Welty. Reprinted by permission of Harvard University Press. Copyright © 1984 by Eudora Welty.

67: Photograph of Alexis Dorenter by Susan Dorenter.

68–69: Photograph by Monica Roberts.

71: "Running Down the Bank" by Dorothea Sharp. Reprinted with permission of The Bridgeman Art Library, Limited.

72–73: Photograph by Monica Roberts. Excerpt from *California and Other States of Grace* by Phyllis Theroux, reprinted by permission of William Morrow and Company, Inc. Copyright 1981 by William Morrow and Company, Inc.

74–75: Photograph by Monica Roberts. Excerpt from *"Thank Heaven for Little Girls"* (From "Gigi") Words by Alan Jay Lerner. Music by Frederick Loewe. Copyright © 1957 and 1958 by Chappell & Co., Inc. International Copyright Secured. All Rights Reserved. Unauthorized copying, arranging, adapting, recording, or public performance is an infringement of copyright. Infringers are liable under the law.

76–77: "Lucy Lavender" from *A Book of a Thousand Poems* by Ivy O. Eastwick. Reprinted by permission of HarperCollins Publishers Limited. "Child with White Cap" by Rose Barton. Reprinted with permission of The Bridgeman Art Library, Limited.

79: Photograph by Alexandra Stonehill.

80–81: Photograph by Monica Roberts.

82: Photograph by Tina Mucci.

84–85: "Madame Charpentier and Her Children" by Pierre Auguste Renoir. Copyright © 1979 The Metropolitan Museum of Art, The Metropolitan Museum of Art, Wolfe Fund, 1907. Catharine Lorillard Wolfe Collection. (07.122). Excerpt from *A Writer's Diary* by Virginia Woolf, copyright 1954, 1953 by Leonard Woolf and renewed 1982, 1981 by Quentin Bell and Angelica Garnett, reprinted by permission of Harcourt Brace Jovanovich, Inc.

86–87: Photograph by Lynn Karlin.

88: Photograph by Penny Gentieu.

90–91: Excerpt from *Winnie-the-Pooh* by A. A. Milne. Copyright 1926 by E.P. Dutton, renewed 1954 by A. A. Milne. Used by permission of the publisher, Dutton Children's Books, a division of Penguin Books USA Inc. Photograph by Monica Roberts.

92: Photograph by Monica Roberts. Excerpt from *Madeline* by Ludwig Bemelmans. Copyright 1939 by Ludwig Bemelmans, renewed © 1967 by Madeleine and Barbara Bemelmans Marciano. Used by permission of the publisher, Viking Penguin, a division of Penguin Books USA Inc.